NOTES ON
Gratitude

BRIAN ROSCOE

NOTES ON GRATITUDE
COPYRIGHT © 2021 BY BRIAN ROSCOE

All rights reserved. No part of this publication may be reproduced, distributed, or transmitted in any form or by any means, including photocopying, recording, or other electronic or mechanical methods, without the prior written permission of the author, except in the case of brief quotations embodied in critical reviews and certain other noncommercial uses permitted by copyright law.

The content of this book is for general informational purposes only. It is not meant to be used, nor should it be used, to diagnose or treat any medical condition or to replace the services of your physician or other healthcare provider. The advice and strategies contained in the book may not be suitable for all readers.

Neither the author, publisher, nor any of their employees or representatives guarantees the accuracy of information in this book or its usefulness to a particular reader, nor are they responsible for any damage or negative consequence that may result from any treatment, action taken, or inaction by any person reading or following the information in this book.

For permission requests or to contact the author, visit:
brianroscoeauthor.com

ISBN-13: 978-1-957348-02-5

PRINTED IN THE UNITED STATES OF AMERICA

NOTES ON
Gratitude

Ahhh, gratitude, gratitude, gratitude. The often forgotten child of love. The healer of our chattering mind, shifter of our destructive attitudes, and opener of hidden doors within our heart. Gratitude helps us see all parts of our life with a new and great attitude, it uncovers understanding when we're confused, and lightens everything that feels heavy and burdensome in our lives. Gratitude: so easy to be pushed to the side in our busy life and yet essential to the fullness of being alive. Gratitude, gratitude, gratitude, thank you for your patience, your undying trust. I do not wish to neglect you. I will write your name on the back of my hand, tattoo you on my mind. Gratitude, let's get to know each other, let's bond, let's get married right now!

"I don't have to chase extraordinary moments to find happiness—it's right in front of me if I'm paying attention and practicing gratitude."
-Brené Brown

Grateful for ALL the Gifts

If we're sensitive, we notice that, as we walk past one another, we're subtly aware of imbalances that exist within and between each other. We might walk past someone and feel an air of negativity, instability, sadness, or anger of some nature—feeling somehow disturbed or disrupted by the frequency and tone of the aberrant energy we've just experienced, not necessarily even being fully aware of what happened, but we know we're feeling something within, something disruptive to our internal world. The truth is, that's just us feeling the energy of our environment. There's nothing to be alarmed about or scared of (assuming violence isn't part of the picture). It helps to see it as more of an information gathering moment for us, and it's important to never take those information gathering sessions personally. They're an ongoing experience for all humans. Our job is to simply allow that momentary experience of someone else's struggle to simply be what it is; to do our best to avoid creating toxic thought or drama around it, and to find a place of compassion to view it from while wishing everyone involved well. It's our way of accepting and blessing life as it moves through us.

As we evolve, we give permission to the universe to use us in whatever way is necessary. We give ourselves permission to become purifiers for the world, to help one another deal with and heal from the effects of the energy generated in the world around us. It helps to remember that we were never promised a pain-free trip, we were just promised growth. Sometimes our greatest gratitude is derived through the trials we've endured to become who we are. **Be grateful for the gifts within the wound.** It's a kindness to ourselves, and it opens up a direct path to knowing, in a very real way, to the core of compassion and forgiveness and how it works through us.

"Gratitude is the healthiest of all human emotions. The more you express gratitude for what you have, the more likely you will have even more to express gratitude for."
-Zig Ziglar

NOTES ON *Gratitude*

If our ultimate goal is to find a *kindness* with one another, what better avenue could there be than *gratitude* and *forgiveness*?

"When I started counting my blessings, my whole life turned around."
-Willie Nelson

The heart of *gratitude* is based in our love for this life.

"It is impossible to feel grateful and depressed in the same moment."
-Naomi Williams

When we're stuck in any kind of negative thinking, gratitude offers us a place to rest and heal. Gratitude helps us return to that quality of precious thought that we all yearn for, thinking that most reflects our truth because it starts from a feeling in the heart. It's not a reflection from the mind. It's reflected to the mind as it moves from the heart upward into our thinking. Gratitude's initial spark comes from a pure place within, it gives the mind the opportunity to begin again, presenting a chance to open to thoughts that heal rather than feeding the thinking that disrupts us. Gratitude adds grace to our thinking and our lives and awakens our heart to the moment in front of us right now.

NOTES ON *Gratitude*

> *"The roots of all goodness lie in the soil of appreciation for goodness."*
> *-Dalai Lama*

Unlived desires, unrealized expectations: like most things in life, they're either greeted by a compassion, an understanding and a gratitude for life, for who we are, who we've become and what we have now, or by the yearning and lament for what we feel we've lost or never received. These are two diametrically opposing responses that impact the human spirit. One depletes life and is a form of self limiting thought, the other opens us up to new possibilities and frees us to move forward. Both are choices.

EXERCISE
Take a minute to define this for yourself, to answer this question: What depletes your ability to have gratitude for life?

What cultivates gratitude in you,
breathes life into it?

"There are only two ways to live your life. One is as though nothing is a miracle. The other is as though everything is a miracle."
-Albert Einstein

Regret has screwed with my life for fifty-six years, and damnit, I'm finally ready to change that!

My goal is to find gratitude for what I am and all I have despite any of life's disappointments, to release myself from past regrets wherever and whenever they pop up, and to be alive and present to where I am right now! My goal is to appreciate whatever moment I find myself in and see this world, my world, as a gift; to consciously sit in deep gratitude of this precious, one-of-a-kind, singular chance to appreciate the gift—a gift meant to open and teach the heart lessons that we can only learn here, as a spirit placed on Earth and tethered to the body of a human being. My goal is to appreciate all that in as many moments as I can.

> *"People with a scarcity mentality tend to see everything in terms of win-lose. There is only so much; and if someone else has it, that means there will be less for me. The more principle-centered we become, the more we develop an abundance mentality, the more we are genuinely happy for the successes, wellbeing, achievements, recognition, and good fortune of other people. We believe their success adds to rather than detracts from our lives."*
> *-Stephen R. Covey*

> *"Reflect upon your present blessings, of which every man has plenty; not on your past misfortunes, of which all men have some."*
> *-Charles Dickens*

Life is inherently driven by love, and everything good, bad or otherwise is initially derived through that love. It's our distortions and disconnect from this truth that encourage ill will within us. But ill will is impossible through the embrace of love.

> *"None is more impoverished than the one who has no gratitude. Gratitude is a currency that we can mint for ourselves, and spend without fear of bankruptcy."*
> *-Fred De Witt Van Amburgh*

There's a freedom derived through life, embracing it, being present to the moment in front of us right now. We just have to grab our opportunity, open to life and its lessons. Those lessons are the gold, they hold our wisdom and our freedom.

Lauren, my oldest daughter, the one that, by myself, I helped deliver. The midwives didn't make it on time, so with angels surrounding us, we bonded as she took her first breath. Yes, that Lauren. She moved away from everyone and everything she knew in Grand Haven, Michigan several years back so she could find herself! Now, I have to say, I thought she should have stayed here, finished up college. But her plans, very plainly, were otherwise. Something spoke to her in Flagstaff, Arizona, and that's where she is as I write this. But Lauren had to leave, I knew that. Something inside her had to go, explore, detach enough from Grand Haven and her parents, grandparents, and everybody that she previously connected with so that she could remember what's most important. She needed to find and remember the deepest part of who she is, remember the heart of Lauren. And that's a process without end, for all of us. When we listen to that whisper, there's no telling where we might end up—in school, out of school, in a great job, wonderful relationship, living in an exciting area of the world we'd never heard of before, or away from all that, immersed in situations we need to struggle through. Our life takes on a design that's quite unexpected when we follow the journey of the heart. And so, for Lauren, it took her to Flagstaff, Arizona.

> *"Each one of us just wants to be noticed and loved and accepted exactly as is— not changed or made different."*
> *-Louise Hay*

NOTES ON *Gratitude*

Leaving to find Lauren. Now that was Lauren's gift to herself, but it was also her gift to me. It forced me to finally get to the place where I simply had to say, "I have no control over this anymore, I have no say in what you do, I have no say in your life and how you live it, whether you live or die is not up to me anymore. Thank you, I love you, and now we are both a little more free." Lauren's leaving impacted me. It took a long time to understand it, but it impacted me and forced me to release any sense of control or responsibility about her life. In her choosing freedom for herself, her strength filtered into my life as well. I can now step back and be her father on a higher level, be her friend and confidant, and just allow her the space to live her life. There's a sadness and a joy in that knowledge, but more than anything, there's growth. And a reclaiming of the self, for both of us.

My most wonderful daughter, Lauren, your life is now and forever will be whatever you want it to be, and it's going to follow the path that you choose. The choices that we make determine the lives that we live. Whatever life becomes or doesn't become, you need to address. It's not about me, your friends, the president, or your religious conviction, because, in the end, you make all the choices, and within that, you drive your life's trajectory.

It's true in everything—divorce, new relationships, jobs—we're responsible for ourselves. That's it. The way we choose to think, the choices we make, will absolutely determine the quality and tone of the lives that we live. And it's inevitably up to us. Only we can make those choices—what to think and how to proceed. I wish you well in your thoughts and your deeds.

NOTES ON *Gratitude*

*"Some people grumble that roses have thorns;
I am grateful that thorns have roses."*
-Alphonse Karr

DEB

Deb, one of my oldest and most dear friends, called me one Sunday very excited about an experience she'd had. She had experienced her own perfect moment of inspiration, which she humorously referred to as, "My evangelical me."

On a sleepless night, she had been struggling with the imminent death of a friend. She found herself asking what she was bringing into the world and leaving behind. Asking herself what the "legacy of Deb" looked like. And in her quiet moment of awakened early morning darkness, she had an authentically personal thought and experience that held her mind and heart tightly.

NOTES ON *Gratitude*

It was a moment of epiphany that was hers alone to be with in that early morning hour. Deb's inspiration had come through her heart, becoming the words that would inspire her to stay on point in her world, to keep walking with a deep breath of aliveness to her life. It was her way of attaching to love's presence. Deb's phrase was "Spread kindness and joy to everyone you meet and give thanks for every day." This was her power statement, meant for her, and true for everyone. It came through her to spark the very soul of who she is.

"Spread kindness and joy to everyone you meet and give thanks for every day" is the statement that puts Deb back on track when she's feeling struggle, attack, and vulnerability. It's what she remembers when she's immersed in gratitude for what she's been given in this life. It's the statement that touches her heart on a moment-to-moment basis, inspiring her toward a quality of life that keeps her grounded and in a state of tenderness and joy. This is Deb's personal definition of love. It's her reminder of who she is.

Statements like this can come through and belong to any of us. We'll choose different words depending on who we are, but it's the essence of the words, the message behind them, that will draw us in toward our heart. Their message will always have a common underlying theme. Remember love, remember your truth. It's how those words speak to our heart and the feelings that they cultivate within us that truly build a picture for us to live by. So now, find that perfect statement that works for you, that inspires you toward your love. Use Deb's if you want, or just explore until the words of your heart unfold for you.

> *"'Enough' is a feast."*
> *-Buddhist proverb*

LAYERS OF Gratitude

The layers of gratitude are expansive. We can find gratitude in whatever experience we encounter in our lives. The only requirement is keeping your eyes open to all the possibilities for it to be experienced in this radical life of ours. We naturally find little gratitudes to feel when we enjoy a special food, drink, or personal activity; tiny pleasures when we're petting a dog, talking to an old friend, or using our new ice maker—the one we've been wanting for years while preparing a meal. These grateful attitudes can spring forward at any moment as we see life with a smile of appreciation. I call these grata-bites, tiny little bite-sized moments of gratitude that are easy to swallow and nurturing for the body.

LITTLE GRATITUDE: the appreciation of the moments of our life, the spontaneous moments of recognition that we have been given a beautiful life. Grata-bites often inspire almost a subconscious moment of breath and a smile. We really like to share these with one another.

And then there's big gratitude! The "I see God" gratitude! The gratitude acknowledging our inspired presence to the world! The gratitude that takes you straight out of your body! Grata-Kong gratitude! Here, you have to stop whatever you're doing because life as you know it shifts. You feel like you can't possibly hold the entirety of what you're experiencing. Suddenly, what you thought was real changes, and the only real thing to you is love and the presence of that miracle in your life. It's a pure masterpiece of inspiration. When you're in Grata-Kong, everyone needs to just leave you alone and let you be in your feelings. It's a show-stopping, prayerful time in which your breath is literally taken away.

Look at all the layers of gratitude as you experience them in your life. Add to this list. You know you're in gratitude when:

- you're sitting in awe, quietly watching something of the world: a baby, children playing, the earth moving around you in some new, previously unseen way, a cloud formed, a sunrise or sunset that catches your breath, a close look at the complexity of an insect, a molecule, a picture of space…

- you find yourself remembering all that your life has inspired in those around you, realized some small purpose of your life as it relates to others…

- you see and realize the many ways your life has been graced, beyond any difficulty and drama, and often the difficulties can even be seen as critical players in your moments of grace…

- you're laughing or crying with a joy that emanates through your very being…

- you're giving freely of yourself without expecting anything in return, receiving only the beauty of your own giving…

- you're able to take joy in the success of others…

- you stop dead in your tracks and stare at the world with awe…

NOTES ON *Gratitude*

- you realize you know a deep, inspired love, and you feel it as it flows through you…

- you find a state of gratitude every time you find a quote that touches you. I, personally, feel grateful that others have been inspired to write them down and share their hearts with the world. I'm struck by the fact of how many of us are working toward the same direction in life, trying to define our deepest understanding of life, to learn the lessons of what it is to be human in this world and surround it with a strength that allows us to know our own hearts…

- you stop for a moment to appreciate a song, a piece of art, the patterns of a floor tile, the grain in a piece of wood, the frozen patterns in a piece of ice…

All of these represent but a tiny portion, a speck, of the many levels of gratitude we can embrace in life.

Essentially, we are blessed with gratitude every time we allow ourselves to be alive to the beauty and awake to the truth that lays behind all of our lives, and present within the gift of living, the gifts already placed in our heart. Gratitude is always, in some way, attached to all that life has to offer, sometimes blatant, often so subtle that they're easily missed. If you want to know gratitude, you need coffee, you have to stay awake to its presence, feel it, and it will come. Gratitude is always there for the taking; it's always there to help us heal our lives.

"He who plants kindness gathers love."
-Saint Basil, the Great (329-379),
Bishop of Cesarea

NOTES ON *Gratitude*

> *"If you count all your assets,
> you always show a profit."*
> -Robert Quillen

Often, the intensity of a challenge roughly relates to the depth and quality of the lesson derived through that challenge.

The universe just wants you to grow, and it doesn't mind compromising your happiness for the moment, giving you a bit of pain and struggle to spark up its lesson, to make sure you know growth is on the table. Sometimes we need an attention grabber, even a stinging slap, and the universe is more than happy to supply. Without the human struggle and drama we encounter in life, we wouldn't have a framework to receive our lessons through. Without that, we would never have the same opportunity to receive the gifts we do. Our lessons have a tendency of coordinating with the intensity of our struggles. It's difficult, but that's what creates a framework for us to grow through. As irrational or contrary to our best interest as that might feel, there's a very real truth to it. Be grateful for your trials. They build character and an ability to grow and move forward in this life. They help you find your strength, and cultivate a sharable compassion, understanding, and ability to love. And that's just unattainable through a life of pure ease.

NOTES ON *Gratitude*

"Acknowledging the good that you already have in your life is the foundation for all abundance."
-Eckhart Tolle

The recognition of any disconnect, any distraction from who we are, the disruption of our truth or wellbeing at any level, is a gift. It's our minds way of saying, "I found something that's not quite working to our benefit, not helping us stay on the old peace train!" It's a natural part of being human that we catch ourselves in this kind of off-centered glitch. In a quiet moment, it's easy to see that within that "lucky catch" lays the miracle of thought and consciousness. In a very real way, it's us participating in life as it flows through us.

After the recognition, the next step, the action to be taken, or the next thought, is in our field. It's our responsibility to move forward from recognizing where we're stuck. And you can either do something with it, or you stay the same. That's pretty much the choice, take it or... take it!

So you ask, *Where's the gratitude in this?* Well, our potential for gratitude lays in having the ability to recognize when we're off track, the grace to self-correct, and having enough self-love to care.

To have that ability to love yourself, to care enough about who you're becoming and to have developed a strength of character that wants to do something about it, well, that's a miracle—a musical of life worth being grateful for, grateful to have, the privilege to participate in this world, in this precious human form. For this, despite the difficulty, we can have gratitude.

NOTES ON *Gratitude*

"You may encounter many defeats, but you must not be defeated. In fact, it may be necessary to encounter the defeats, so you can know who you are, what you can rise from, how you can still come out of it."
−Maya Angelou

"Gratitude turns what we have into enough, and more. It turns denial into acceptance, chaos into order, confusion into clarity... it makes sense of our past, brings peace for today, and creates a vision for tomorrow."
−Melody Beattie

PUTTING ON THE WORST-CASE-SCENARIO LENS!

Sometimes I have a hard time getting into a space were gratitude can weave its way into my thinking. I know it's happening because I catch myself feeling and usually acting stupid-grouchy with little reason. When I see it, I'll step back and try a grateful attitude reboot. Depending on what's stuck in my head in the moment, I might use the worst-case-scenario lens to look at life. I consider the topic I think has me in a bad mood, and then I look at all the ways it could exist in my life—all the things that could have happened that are less desirable than what I'm dealing with in the moment. I look at all that could have gone wrong or been born wrong in that scenario, and it helps me step back and put things in a better perspective so I can appreciate what I have now. It helps me walk forward from a place of gratitude. That may or may not play a role in how things change, but it sure plays a role in how I change. It allows me to see even the things I don't care for with more grace, see my life as "just right," like Goldilock's porridge.

For example, I might not like the house I live in, but I look at a worst-case-scenario. I look for a scenario that allows me to see all that I have, make space to appreciate where I am in the moment. *I've lost my house in a fire, or it went back to the bank, or I live in a war-torn country...* need I say more?

Using the worst-case-scenario technique when we encounter difficult life experiences helps us find gratitude for all the other possibilities life presents us and an appreciation for what it has spared us from.

Considering the worst case scenario helps you step back from your dance with impending doom and lets you know you're going to be okay, you can handle life, you just need to get okay with being okay—to be where we are, happy for the opportunity to be alive, trusting our process, and feeling enough, lovable, and loved. Like most of our lessons, knowing gratitude is more about being immersed in moving in its direction, learning more and more about how it impacts our lives, not necessarily arriving at some final destination.

> *"The world has enough beautiful mountains and meadows, spectacular skies and serene lakes. It has enough lush forests, flowered fields, and sandy beaches. It has plenty of stars and the promise of a new sunrise and sunset every day. What the world needs more of is people to appreciate and enjoy it."*
> -Michael Josephson

NOTES ON *Gratitude*

When we come to the realization that some of the attitudes that we hold as true, perhaps even set in stone, ideas that we may have thought were important but on examination seem to be holding us back from exploring ourselves, from knowing our truth, it allows us to see two directions in our life more clearly:

A. We can step back and observe the world we used to live in, our past beliefs, the old thinking we previously called home. It's a place we inhabited, that, for a time, may have been useful to us, but now has become inefficient, obsolete and irrelevant in our world today.

B. We get a deeper sense, a vision, of where we might go, who we might become. We see the directions yet to be fully explored, and although different and scary, we recognize that they're exciting and alive to us as well. We get a glimpse into a new, more fulfilling way to think, and within that, if we choose,to live.

"Gratitude is a currency that we can mint for ourselves, and spend without fear of bankruptcy."
-Fred de Witt Van Amburgh

Gratitude's one of the big kahunas on this journey—a quality of being definitely worth striving for. It's one of the major intersections on that big highway of love, and it helps all other qualities of love come alive and unite in a stronger way within us. It's like the crazy glue of the heart! Gratitude helps us put a better, more robust spin on everything we truly desire on this journey, it brightens all the goals of the heart. Whatever we touch in life with gratitude as our partner has a strength attached that did not formally exist. Gratitude builds in a strength of heart to all circumstances and ideas of life.

We have to get down and dirty with gratitude, explore the qualities of what it is to open to it and own its presence in us. We need to ask the big defining questions of the heart: So what does this internal state of gratitude look like? Can we put our thoughts and feelings into words, explaining its presence in our hearts and what influence it has over our lives? What does it look like in our minds, feel like in our hearts, and who do we become when gratitude shines through us? How do we see and relate to others? How do we see ourselves? What becomes of our self-talk and struggle? What new ways of being are created within us, ideas of living with more truth, when we are awake to the gift of gratitude? Who do we become when we employ the gratitude that naturally flows through us, when we uncover the emotional shrouds and distracting ideas that keep us so sleepy to this gift of being?

There are folks out there telling you to have gratitude, explaining what having gratitude does for you, all the biblical and religious teachings that point you in gratitude's direction. But how about when you're not in a state of gratitude? How do you get there? Where are your gratitude training wheels? What do you do to attain that which you most desire? How do you find that spark when you're stuck in a life that sometimes seems nothing short of difficult and disastrous?

There's information out there about gratitude, but what it is to actually have and live in gratitude? That's a whole other story to explore. Explaining it is like explaining life itself—when we try to explain life's fullness, we come to the conclusion that the bigness of it is, indeed, ineffable. There are no words, it's so deep that it has to exist free of words and held as a heartfelt feeling, a spark of light.

People, however, study and try to expound on gratitude and its benefits. They've found that the benefits people derive from living with deep unbinding gratitude for life are evident in the enhanced quality of our personal relationships, the tendency to better maintain the physical healthcare we're worthy of, enhanced psychological health, emotional balance, maintaining a quality of exercise we enjoy and our bodies respond well to, getting the quality of sleep we need, deeper feelings of self-worth and belonging, and a stronger intellect and mental acuity as we participate in life. You can read about it in a book, but you really can't feel it from those pages. You need to take the journey of owning and preciously embodying it. Being in gratitude requires your emersion in life. It requires you to see life beyond the explainable. It requires you to breathe into the ineffable miracle of all that surrounds you. It's a feel-it-first opportunity, and then, perhaps, try-to-explain-it kind of thing. This is because it initiates from and through your heart first, well before it ever hits your head.

Gratitude finds its origins in the heart, it begins in the heart and quickly flows into the ideas of the mind. So when we are presented with the word "gratitude," we often just smile. We don't even know why, we don't necessarily need an idea. We're just grateful for life, and gratitude has already been planted within us, we just need to access it.

> *"The way to develop the best that is in a person is by appreciation and encouragement."*
> -Charles Schwab

NOTES ON *Gratitude*

Everything in our lives is temporary. All dramas, thoughts, feelings, personalized troubles of any kind—they're all temporary. Unless, of course, we decide to hold onto something longer than that, turn it into a marathon. However, no matter how long we choose to hold it, that's also temporary, because, after all, we're kind of temporary, too. It's probably easier spending your time in gratitude for what is rather than attaching your life flow to what was.

"He is a wise man who does not grieve for the things which he has not, but rejoices for those which he has."
-Epictetus

Age often comes with its gifts and its wisdom, its given insights that us youngins just tend to overlook.

Anna is an older patient in the practice, about eighty-seven years old. She's in great shape, one of those people who never seems to mentally age. One morning before a treatment, she sat down on the table, looked me in the eye, and said with conviction, *"Doc, you know, there's a lot of healing in gratitude, it just seems to relate to everything around me. If I throw some gratitude at it, it heals. It's really quite amazing."*

Well, that was enough for me to pay attention, it inspired me to start exploring gratitude more for myself. Anna was right. Gratitude is quite amazing, and what would we be with the absence of gratitude in our lives? How would we open the doors of our heart? What healing would we have to give up without gratitude in our human toolbox? Could we heal or could we even exist without gratitude in our world? Personally, I don't think so.

"Let us rise up and be thankful, for if we didn't learn a lot today, at least we learned a little, and if we didn't learn a little, at least we didn't get sick, and if we got sick, at least we didn't die; so, let us all be thankful."
-Buddha

Spend some time exploring the ideas and research around this *gratitude phenomenon:*

- First, look at the teachings that encourage gratitude in us as individuals and society as a whole.

- Second, what's the research out there that supports how gratitude benefits us physically, emotionally, spiritually, and as a culture?

- Third, and perhaps most important, how do we transition ourselves from a life without gratitude to the ability to embrace it? Life that's, perhaps, shrouded in negativity and even a victim mentality to a life that allows us to immerse ourselves in gratitude, that allows us to find a personal definition for gratitude and how it impacts our lives, and embrace a state of being that allows gratitude in and encourages it and recognizes it in as many ways as we're able. How do we transition into a life that reboots the very framework of life as we know it and welcomes gratitude where it was previously unknown or unwelcome.

If you really want something, research it, understand it, do your best to own it.

GRATITUDE QUESTIONS:

- How does gratitude support me?
- How does the lack of gratitude affect me?
- What does that do?
- How does it feel?
- Who do I become?

Gratitude. I don't know if gratitude on its own actually does anything. It needs us. Unless we put it into action, it just sits there, staring at us like a hungry dog, wagging its tail, waiting for recognition. But gratitude is a natural expression of our true nature—it seems to want to be a part of what we're meant to be, to contribute to the quality of being we're asked to explore and embody. To the best of my knowledge, there aren't many teachings out there telling us to avoid gratitude at any cost! So, I think we can safely assume gratitude has a little something going for it. It seems then, we're left with the option to embrace gratitude if we choose, and allow its benefits to spill forward into our lives.

With gratitude in our pocket, suddenly, we're able to appreciate more of life, to explore how love can unfold into everything we think and do. Gratitude is one with love, one with forgiveness, and over time, it naturally gets recognized for its value as we evolve more and more into ourselves, into and through our hearts. Through this, we find our truth as beings of light, beings that just happen to have bodies, apparently just to complicate things, but nevertheless beings that can know love.

> *"Piglet noticed that even though he had a very small heart, it could hold a rather large amount of gratitude."*
> *-A.A. Milne*

Cultivating gratitude requires a very real dedication to ourselves, a bit of practice, and the willingness to expand beyond what we think we can feel, some self-belief and a knowing that we play the ultimate role in determining the quality of our life experience, owning the purity of self-love, understanding that love is all powerful and its essence allows us to stretch beyond any of our fears. Gratitude requires us to acknowledge that the internal quality of our existence is profound evidence that we are love and loved. It's the last part, knowing that we are loved, that needs to be embraced internally. Knowing that we're loved is a big feat, one that we have to find our own, very individual way of seeing. It's true for all of us. It's just that not all of us can necessarily see it that easily. This is perhaps due to the religious dogma we've acquired, or the current state of our life situation, or just a tendency not to trust the world or ourselves. But it doesn't require a religion, and it doesn't require a belief system to know we're emerged in a love that requires nothing but our recognition. It simply requires an opening up to our truth. It's a kind of rationalization we find inside ourselves, simply because we are here, in this miracle, given a body and mind, freedom to determine our thinking, regardless of our circumstances, a freedom that's impossible to remove from our essence. This is love, this is the gift, even though parts of our experience might suck. Therefore, we accept this gift as one of love. Our situations won't always be ideal, but our presence in this world is, and all we ever have for real is the love that we recognize within and help bring forward through connection to our heart.

"Forget yesterday—it has already forgotten you. Don't sweat tomorrow—you haven't even met. Instead, open your eyes and your heart to a truly precious gift—today."
-Steve Maraboli

NOTES ON *Gratitude*

At some point, while writing *Inspirational Espresso*, it occurred to me how huge this love concept was for us to take into our world. To help myself grasp the vastness of this love, I found myself developing a concept I called "The Holon of Love." It was based in the idea that love, like the universe, is made up of infinite parts—the biggest parts of love, we're aware of, and the tiniest ones, probably not. But the particles all reflect the exact same reflection as the whole. When we separate one part, such as kindness, generosity, forgiveness, compassion, understanding, gratitude, they all have within them the essence of the other. They all reflect every other part of love's presence in the whole. In essence, they are not only part of love, they are, indeed, the whole of love.

If you can't find the wherewithal to be grateful, practice other forms of love and they will naturally lead you toward gratitude over time.

The idea of holon is best described as something that is simultaneously a whole and a part, simultaneously a whole in itself and, at the same time, is nested within another holon, making it a part of something much larger than itself. Thus, the holon of love suggests that all branches of love are simultaneously a part of love and reflect the whole of love. The parts of love cannot exist outside of the presence of the others, and naturally come together to make up something much larger than themselves. The word "love" is the most commonly used word for this phenomena of being, however, even love ceases to exist without the presence of its congruent parts. Without compassion, understanding and kindness, love is not. The same is conversely true for all qualities of love. Love is given to us as a larger than life itself gift to embrace on this human journey of ours.

No matter what quality of love you practice, when it's done with a pure heart, it will bring you closer to gratitude. That's the nature of love. It builds on itself, no matter what the form. It's a holon.

Gratitude naturally exists in all other forms of *love*.

"In ordinary life, we hardly realize that we receive a great deal more than we give, and that it is only with gratitude that life becomes rich."
-Dietrich Bonhoeffer

Love is a gift to all humans. Everyone has it available to them at any point in their lives. The only trick is, we have to choose it. Love covers all the bases, everything! All events, predicaments, struggles, joys can be integrated with love. If you're having a hard time connecting with gratitude, touch another part of love, explore that, spend some time there and it allows gratitude to evolve, it helps it come out of its shell. Then try exploring it again.

> *"I truly believe we can either see the connections, celebrate them, and express gratitude for our blessings, or we can see life as a string of coincidences that have no meaning or connection. For me, I'm going to believe in miracles, celebrate life, rejoice in the views of eternity, and hope my choices will create a positive ripple effect in the lives of others. This is my choice."*
> -Mike Ericksen

www.ingramcontent.com/pod-product-compliance
Lightning Source LLC
Chambersburg PA
CBHW022231080526
44577CB00005B/174